BASIC LEGAL CONCEPTS

Basic Legal Concepts for the Non-Lawyer

by

John D. Ferrell

BASIC LEGAL CONCEPTS

CONTRACTS

The most important and basic concept in contract law is that of *consideration*. A contract is not binding unless there is consideration for it. This means something of value must be given under the contract arrangement from each side—such as money on one side, and a product from the other; or money for services, or services for services, or a product for another product from the other side. The basic idea is that of an exchange of one thing for another thing.

The law does not look at the *adequacy* of the consideration being given for what is obtained. Thus, it is common to see documents recite that a contract is being entered into "for one dollar [sometimes, ten dollars] and other good and valuable consideration", even when the value on the other side is in the hundreds of millions. A court is not supposed to examine the adequacy of consideration, from the standpoint of contract law. Of course, if a deal is grossly unfair to one side or the other, the

BASIC LEGAL CONCEPTS

court might invalidate the contract as a fraud. But fraud is difficult to prove in courts.

Contractual arrangements, or obligations, may arise from certain documents that follow a prescribed format—such as a check or a promissory note. These are limited purpose instruments, and not open to covering subjects outside the limited scope of the transaction of payment, or the incurring of a financial obligation. Sometimes people will try to add something important in the Memorandum space at the bottom of a check in order to clarify a contractual arrangement, or to impose some additional obligation on the payee of the check. These additions do not in any way alter the payment obligation arising under the check. A court may consider the addition as a notation as evidencing to some extent the parties' intent regarding the underlying transaction, but the notation has no effect on the payment obligation, and banks can process the check without regard to the notation, as if it had never been made—debiting the check-drawer's account without regard to the notation.

At earlier times in the development of the common law, contracts had to be sealed by the parties in order to be binding (or in some states, the contract under seal was an alternative to one where consideration had to be shown). By now, most States have adopted statutes that expressly state that a seal is totally without legal significance and has no effect on whether the document is binding. Notwithstanding theses statutes, most corporations that enter into an important contract will have the authorized officer who signs the contract on behalf of the corporation affix the corporate seal next to the signature. The final line before the signatures on a contract is customarily that "the parties have hereunto set their hands and seals

BASIC LEGAL CONCEPTS

this____ day of _____, 2013"—even if the parties do not in fact affix their seals.

A recent book entitled "Debt: The First 5,000 Years" by David Graeber argues that contractual obligations in traditional societies, both historically and at present, arise because of long-standing traditional relationships between the parties, such as a history of personal favors, or kinship relations, or relationships of dominance and subservience between various villages, etc. When I was a child in a rural area, if one farmer helped another one with something difficult, such as loading a heavy object onto his truck, the one who had been helped would say, "Much obliged", which meant, "I am very obligated to you" and this suggested that the favor would be repaid at some future date. In Portuguese, the word is "obrigado", which has all the same connotations as the English counterpart. At its lowest level, this is just a polite way of saying,"Thank you."

What we are dealing with in this book is not how people come to feel obligated, but what it takes in the law to make a contract fully binding. The main determinant is whether there is consideration supporting it. States adopting the Uniform Commercial Code, now adopted in all States in one form or another, impose an additional requirement that the contract be in writing if it involves more than a certain sum of money in value. Typically, where there is a writing requirement applicable to the case, the party suing on the contract must be prepared to present an original, signed version of the contract to the court.

BASIC LEGAL CONCEPTS

CRIMINAL LAW

The most important concept in criminal law is that of *mens rea*. This Latin term is taken from a Latin phrase meaning "the act is not guilty unless the mind is also guilty." Literally, *mens rea* means "guilty mind." This does not mean the person must feel guilty. Rather, it means he must have intended to commit the bad act.

This concept is perhaps best illustrated in the old case of Fain v. Kentucky. In this case a customer had fallen asleep in a barber chair at the local barber shop. When closing time came, a worker at the barber shop woke him up, whereupon the customer drew his pistol and shot him dead. The customer was initially convicted of murder, but the conviction was overturned on appeal. There had been no showing that he had formed any intention to kill or harm anyone. He was coming out of the fog of sleep and didn't know what he was doing. The court found there was no *mens rea*.

In many cases, the guilty mind will be presumed from the act itself. The Fain case is unusual because of the sleep factor. If a person commits securities fraud, we can usually presume that he knew the facts relating to the various elements of the crime, e.g., he knew the shares sold were not registered securities, he knew that the purchasers had relied on his representation that they were registered, he knew that there was no available exemption from the Federal securities laws, etc. *Mens rea* is not as important an issue in cases such as this.

Under 18 USC sec.3142, applicable in the Federal courts, a defendant will generally be granted bail, if the defendant is likely to show up for trial or is not likely to endanger the safety

BASIC LEGAL CONCEPTS

of witnesses or of the community. If there is an issue on one of these two points, bail may still be granted but at an increased amount. In State courts, bail may be granted "as of right", or in the discretion of the court, depending on the nature of the case. Since there is no absolute right to bail, as a practical matter, bail is always in the discretion of the court.

In modern criminal law practice, a significant portion of the issues raised are constitutional law issues, which will be covered in a later section. Many criminal cases involve the Fourth Amendment [freedom from unreasonable searches and seizures] or the Fifth Amendment [the privilege against self-incrimination; guaranty of due process of law] to the Constitution.

Different rules of statutory interpretation apply in reading criminal statutes than in reading civil statutes. The narrowest reading of a criminal statute is required, and only conduct that is clearly and unquestionably prohibited should be deemed a crime. Some statutes, such as the tax code, which are a mixture of criminal and civil provisions, present difficult problems of statutory interpretation. The tax code has become almost unreadable to anyone who is not a tax specialist. It is drafted in a style that is intended to be incredibly precise, but instead is just incredible.

TORTS

There are two categories of torts: intentional torts, and torts based on negligence. Negligence torts are committed by someone who owes a duty of care to the person who has been harmed by negligence, doctor-patient, lawyer-client, or even

BASIC LEGAL CONCEPTS

where the duty of care is more generalized, as where both parties are members of the same general community, as one car-driver to another. A tort is a civil harm, not a crime, which usually can be compensated only by money damages. Often, insurance plays a role in covering the harm.

One important tort action is becoming almost impossible to prove. Libel (or defamation), which may be either intentional or negligent, of a person found to be a public figure has become impossible, and the definition of who is a public figure is becoming broader and broader.

The people generally who most need to be able to bring a libel action are celebrities, public officials and others now considered public figures under the libel laws. The very people who most need protection are unable to have recourse to a libel action. The destruction of the libel tort action began with the case of NY Times v. Sullivan (1964). The facts of the case were that the Times ran an advertisement that was filled with factual inaccuracies about actions of the Montgomery, Ala. Police. The Public Safety Commissioner there, who supervised the police, sued the Times for libel. Alabama law at that time required a libel plaintiff to send a request to the paper asking for a retraction before a public official could pursue a libel action. Mr. Sullivan did that, and the Times refused to print a retraction of the factual errors. The US Supreme Court ruled that permitting a libel action here by a public official would unconstitutionally interfere with freedom of speech guaranteed by the First Amendment. This concept has been extended far beyond the facts of governmental action that were involved in the Sullivan case. What public purpose would be served in preventing someone like Halle Berry from suing for false statements made by some trashy magazine about her personal

BASIC LEGAL CONCEPTS

life? The glorious aims of the First Amendment are certainly not brought to mind in cases such as this. The difficulty is that courts do not do well in drawing distinctions between qualities of free speech involved in various libel cases. I am sure that Mr. Sullivan felt that the Times was equally trashy in refusing to retract its factual errors in the newspaper.

Some conservative politicians have been pushing something they call "tort reform", which means exempting doctors and hospitals from the consequences of their negligent or even intentional harmful acts to their patients. Most States that have followed the lead of the AMA have taken a somewhat more modest step—although that step has the same practical effect as the blanket exemption from liability. Some States such as New Jersey require a so-called "affidavit of merit" from another medical professional before a malpractice case can proceed; most doctors are unwilling to give an affidavit that could be used against another doctor—no matter how horrendous the harm to the patient who is victimized by the medical malpractice. They feel their duty to other doctors is higher than any duty to a patient. The highest courts in the States of Arkansas and Oklahoma have invalidated their "affidavit of merit" statutes as violative of their State Constitutions, using a clause that is in almost all State Constitutions and is in concept similar to the Equal Protection Clause in the Federal Constitution. In the State Constitutions, it is referred to as the prohibition on any "special law". The "affidavit of merit" statute treats people in certain occupations differently from others when they are tort defendants. Imagine a situation where a bank is precluded from suing a person who robbed the bank to recover its property unless the bank first gets an affidavit of merit from another bank-robber. To say the least,

BASIC LEGAL CONCEPTS

this forces a victim-plaintiff to get the assistance of someone who has an identity of interest with the defendant side.

The politicians pushing so-called "tort reform" are claiming it will lower medical costs. But who is to say that having more patients die or become gravely ill from incompetent or negligent medical treatment by doctors and hospitals will actually reduce medical costs. Clearly some costs would be transferred from doctors and hospitals to patients by denying adequate compensation. But incentivizing incompetence and negligence by medical professionals cannot be a good solution from a public policy standpoint.

THE CONSTITUTION: STRUCTURE OF GOVERNMENT

The purpose of any constitution is primarily to lay out the structure of government, such as the roles of the legislative, executive, and judicial branches, and the powers of the national government. In a Federal system such as in the US, it is necessary to describe to some degree the responsibilities of the State governments vis-à-vis the Federal government. Ordinarily it is not a place for laying out the rights of individual citizens. The US Constitution itself did not do so, but this created huge political problems for ratification in Virginia, the geographically largest and most populous State. If Virginia did not ratify, there was no chance of the new Constitution going into effect. Thomas Jefferson had been through this battle in Virginia over having a bill of rights, at the State level. Hamilton and Madison were the principal architects of the Constitution. And Hamilton in particular was a purist, and did not want any part of the

BASIC LEGAL CONCEPTS

Constitution devoted to individual rights. Madison was by nature more flexible and, like Jefferson, was from Virginia and understood the political problem there. Madison and Jefferson worked out a plan to offer a bill of rights, as the first ten amendments to the Constitution, which would be offered for ratification at the same time as the Constitution itself. In this way, they preserved the ratifications of the Constitution itself in those States that had already acted. They were very concerned that not enough States would ratify it, and this compromise ensured that the necessary number of States would be reached.

There was another way this matter could have been resolved. The primary group in Virginia pushing for a bill of rights was the Baptists, whose main concern was to see that the Episcopal Church [the descendant of the Church of England] did not become the established church for the nation. If the main body of the Constitution had included a ban on having an established church, It would have passed in that form in all States. (The ban on having an established church was included in the First Amendment.) Even Hamilton would have agreed that the issue of an established church was a structural issue of government that could have been addressed in the main text of a Constitution. We have probably all benefited from having a full list of individual rights enshrined in constitutional law--even if politically it could have been avoided.

Many people believe that the US Supreme Court is the last word on all legal issues in this country. It is the last word on all issues of Federal law, including Constitutional law. However, most issues that arise in the courts in the country are issues of State law. State law includes much more than the State constitution and State statutes passed by the State legislature and approved by the governor. The common law, coming down from

BASIC LEGAL CONCEPTS

centuries of practice in the English courts constitutes the background against which all issues are considered. The common law rule on a particular matter may be superseded by a State or Federal statute. But most garden-variety cases in torts or contracts, etc. are decided by the common law, as it is interpreted in the particular State. The Federal Constitution only establishes the role of the *Federal* courts. The State courts are established and governed by the State laws. For example, the Federal Constitution establishes lifetime tenure for Federal judges, but has no impact on the tenures of State court judges, which are normally not lifetime.

Most cases that go up to the US Supreme Court contain a mixture of different types of issues, State and Federal, Constitutional, statutory or common law. The Court has adopted a rule for not wasting its time on matters where it is not the ultimate arbiter. It does not wish to consider appeals where there is an "adequate State ground." (Strictly speaking, an 'appeal' to the Court is when the case goes up "as of right"; when a review is undertaken by the Court in its discretion that is on a "petition for certiorari".) This means that if the judgment in the court below could properly rest on a reason based on State law, it will decline to consider the case. Thus, for example, if there is a question where a conviction in the court below was originally based on an unreasonable search and seizure, and an intermediate appeals court found that the search had violated the State statute governing the procedure for doing governmental searches, the Supreme Court will not reexamine the State law question or reach a decision based on its interpretation of the 4th Amendment to the Federal Constitution.

BASIC LEGAL CONCEPTS

A review of the cases presented to the Supreme Court in any year will demonstrate to anyone that this truly is a Federal system: numerous issues of State action and State law are intertwined with Federal matters. To make things more complex, several Amendments to the Federal Constitution adopted after the Civil War were directed to the States to deal with the treatment of former slaves. The 14th Amendment guarantees due process of law and the Equal Protection of the Laws to all citizens, not just former slaves, directed against State action. (The Fifth Amendment guarantees due process of law in Federal proceedings; the 14th A. guarantees it in State proceedings.) This Amendment also made all former slaves citizens if they were born or naturalized in the US.

REGULATORY SYSTEMS

There are other bodies of law applicable to a citizen besides constItutions, statutes, and the common law. There are rules imposed by a regulatory agency to implement a particular statute, which is within the agency's area of authority. Thus, the FDA may adopt rules relating to drugs, but not to air traffic control, etc.

Generally, agencies have at least two levels of rules:(a) regulations, which generally lay out the regulatory scheme implementing a particular statute, defining terms not otherwise defined in the statute, often setting out the enforcement procedure that will be used in carrying out the statute and regulation, (b) 'rulings', which by their terms usually relate only to one citizen or taxpayer, although because it is a precedent,

BASIC LEGAL CONCEPTS

the ruling has the practical effect of being of general applicability. (Sometimes, rulings are drafted to be of general applicability.) Rulings are generally far more numerous than regulations; the IRS regulations are usually printed in two paperback volumes, the entire rulings and regulations are printed in many, many loose-leaf volumes, with many more pages devoted to rulings than to regulations. Regulations and rulings are invalid if they are in conflict with the underlying statute in any respect; their role is simply to carry out the purposes of the statute.

One major problem in the regulatory area is in determining which agency has the authority to adopt rules relating a particular question. A couple of examples from the bank regulatory area can illustrate this point. First, it is important to know that the Comptroller of the Currency {an agency within the Department of the Treasury] regulates national banks, and that the Federal Reserve Board regulates, among other things, State-chartered banks that are members of the Federal Reserve System. There was a statute setting out the powers of national banks adopted in the 1860's, and the Federal Reserve Act in 1913 made this statute applicable to State member banks in order to keep them on the same regulatory footing. There was a Comptroller in the early 1960's who was very favorably inclined toward national banks; this Comptroller issued a ruling interpreting the statute that was a sharp departure from prior interpretations and taking a much broader view of the powers of national banks. The Fed responded by issuing a ruling that the Comptroller's ruling was totally without any legal foundation, and could not be relied on by State member banks. The second dispute that can serve as an example, occurred in the 1970's involving national banks that engage in foreign activities. The Comptroller, as the primary supervisor of

BASIC LEGAL CONCEPTS

national banks, usually determines what is adequate capital for a national bank. The Fed regulates the overseas activities of national banks and State member banks. The Fed often imposed capital requirements on a bank applying for permission to make a foreign acquisition or carry on a new activity overseas. The Fed told a very large national bank that it needed more capital to do what was being proposed. The Comptroller responded that he was the sole decider of the appropriate level of capital for a national bank. Naturally, the Fed rejected this position.

Conflicts such as this are inevitable in the bank regulatory area because of the multiple agencies, FDIC, Comptroller and Fed and for savings and loans, the FHLBB. The statutes are also tangled and confusing. Other agencies have similar problems. The FAA and CAB both regulate air traffic and aircraft—but they seem to have sorted out their jurisdictional boundaries much better.

At one time, the SEC was often in conflict with the banking agencies. Although the line between investment banks and commercial banks has become blurred, because of the effective repeal of the Glass-Steagall Act from 1933, there has not been much talk in recent years about conflicts between the agencies. Previously, banks used to agitate to have their bank holding company securities regulated by the Fed, which regulates bank holding companies; bank securities' issuances have been regulated for quite some time by the banking agencies. Federal Reserve Regulation F governs the securities of State member banks; it would not require a major effort to convert this to covering bank holding companies as well. The Fed regulates margin requirements, which sets the amount of collateral that must be held on loans secured by stocks or other types of

BASIC LEGAL CONCEPTS

securities, for all lenders; the Fed's margin regulation contains a definition of the term 'security', and the SEC rules also define this term.

At present, the area most open for conflict between the SEC and another agency, would seem to be that involving the Commodity Futures Trading Commission—now that the CFTC is regulating swaps (since the Dodd-Frank Act). It would seem that the time is long overdue for straightening out the jurisdictional issues relating to financial regulation. Lax regulatory oversight has been identified as a principal cause of the financial collapse and the continuing recession.

BASIC LEGAL CONCEPTS

SUBSTANTIVE LAW VS. PROCEDURAL LAW: Remedies for Constitution Violations

Often, there are portions of the Constitution or of a statute that establishes a substantive right, but the provision of law granting the substantive right is not on its face self-executing. The court must then fashion a remedy that will preserve the substantive right. The 4th Amendment guarantees freedom from unreasonable searches and seizures. The Court, if it finds the search unreasonable, without probable cause, it will preclude the introduction of the drugs that were stored under your bed. Your lawyer can file a motion to suppress, which if granted, will prevent the evidence from being used against you in any prosecution. Procedural law covers those legal matters that enable your substantive right to be realized. It will also cover those areas that guide the prosecution in obtaining a proper warrant for a search, etc., what is probable cause for issuing a warrant and so.

Sometimes a statute is found to be arbitrarily discriminatory against certain persons, in violation of either the due process clause or the Equal Protection clause of the Fourteenth Amendment or the due process clause of the 5th Amendment. The Court normally invalidates the statute as the remedy; it does not attempt to re-draft the statute in order to make it not in violation. In that situation, the legislative branch must pass a new statute that has been cleaned up so that it contains no violations.

BASIC LEGAL CONCEPTS

BUSINESS ENTITIES

The simplest form in which one can carry on a business is that of a sole proprietorship, which is simply the individual wearing his business hat. Even banks in Europe can be organized as a sole proprietorship, and known by the name of the owner, such as the Julius Baer Bank. The most common forms of organization for any sizeable business are usually the corporation and the partnership.

There are several advantages and some disadvantages to the corporate form of ownership. A corporation engaged in business may be sued, but its shareholders ordinarily are not liable for obligations of the corporation. There are certain exceptions to this, where the so-called "corporate veil" is pierced and liability is imposed on shareholders; this will usually occur only where the legal niceties of corporate organization have not been followed. A corporation must have a board of directors, which is supposed to exercise independent judgment from that of its shareholders and corporate management; under corporation law, the board is often charged with "managing the affairs" of the corporation.

A partnership can be organized by the owners of a business, who are all called partners. A corporate entity may be a partner in a partnership. There are two main forms of partnership: a general partnership, and a limited partnership. A general partnership has all general partners, all of whom have unlimited liability for obligations of the partnership. A limited partnership must have at least one general partner who manages the

BASIC LEGAL CONCEPTS

partnership. The limited partners have no right to manage the business of the partnership, but do receive a specified portion of the net income of the partnership; limited partners have liability only to the extent of the capital they have contributed to the partnership. Under US tax law, a partnership itself is not taxed, but the income is deemed distributed to the partners and taxed to the partners individually. A partner pays tax on his portion of partnership income, whether or not it is actually distributed to him.

Under the US tax code, a corporation may elect to be taxed under Subchapter S, which is the same as for a partnership. A Subchapter S corporation must have only individual shareholders; this is a very important limitation, since it prevents an institutional investor from buying into such a corporation. In such a situation, the corporation must either withdraw its Subchapter S election or change its business form.

In recent years, a new form of organization has become popular: the limited liability company, or LLC. In an LLC, the owners are shielded from unlimited liability. The company does not have shares; the owners are called "members", not shareholders. The LLC usually sets up a "board of managers", which may or may not include members on this board. The company is ordinarily taxed like a partnership. The membership agreement will ordinarily describe the capital contributions and allocated portions of income for each member.

The LLC has the benefit of limited liability like a corporation, and the benefit of "flow-through" taxation like a partnership. On its face it would seem that the LLC would be a good choice for a form of business organization. But both partnerships and corporations have had many centuries of legal practice; as a

BASIC LEGAL CONCEPTS

result, almost every conceivable legal issue relating to them has been considered in the courts and been resolved, with the answer able to be known by the practicing lawyer. The LLC is relatively untested in the courts. Can certain actions of the members of an LLC raise the issues of "piercing the corporate veil" that come up in the case of corporations. What happens if the board of managers takes actions that are not in the best interest of the member-owners?

PRACTICE APPLICABLE TO INDIVIDUAL CLIENTS

Individual client practice is mostly directed to wills, trusts and estates. First, we will begin with wills. The legal requirements applicable to wills vary from State to State. Some States require two witnesses, some require three, some require none if the will is "holographic" [written entirely in the handwriting of the person executing the will].Usually, the will begins with a title at the top of the first page saying"LAST WILL AND TESTAMENT". The first paragraph begins:

> I, John Q. Doe, hereby declare and publish this to be my last will and testament. I hereby give, devise and bequeath as follows:

BASIC LEGAL CONCEPTS

Next, follow several numbered paragraphs [numbered in text like FIRST, SECOND, etc.] stating who gets what. The first few contain bequests of specific amounts of money or specific objects; next comes the ones for specific individuals. The final paragraph of bequests is the one for the residuary [whatever is left after the specific bequests are deducted]. The residuary paragraph first sentence begins "All the rest, residue and remainder of my estate I give, devise and bequeath to".

The bulk of most estates is made up of homes, which are commonly in the name of the husband and wife; title to this real estate in joint name passes outside the will to the surviving spouse.

Some States have special rules to protect the widow. New Jersey permits the surviving spouse to elect against the will and obtain one-third of the estate if the husband and wife have not been living separate and apart for the last six months before death. There is a limit on the time within which the surviving spouse must file a complaint to elect against the will.

Trusts may be created under a will—called testamentary trusts—or among the living—called *inter vivos* trusts. Trusts may be revocable by the grantor or irrevocable. For revocable trusts, the assets are considered in the estate of the grantor for estate tax purposes; even the income is taxable to the grantor. Trusts are a way of segregating certain assets and identifying them as being for the benefit of named persons or charities. The trust is effective in disposing of the identified assets. The revocable trust is mostly desired by people who are not sure if they will have enough assets or income to live on in old age, and may need to take the assets back when needed.

BASIC LEGAL CONCEPTS

ACQUISITION OF A BUSINESS

There are several methods of acquiring a business. The two most common are: (1) acquisition of the stock of the company; and (2) acquisition of assets of the business. The decision of which to use is often dictated by tax considerations. In an acquisition of assets, it may be possible to get a step-up in the tax basis of the assets, enabling the buyer to depreciate the assets at a higher rate against income, shielding some future income from taxation. However, in an asset acquisition, it may be necessary to comply with all the formalities of the bulk sales act, which is a uniform act in effect States throughout the US, and in the provinces of Canada. The bulk sales act is intended to protect creditors of the company being acquired. The statute is often ignored when a very credit-worthy seller gives a blanket indemnity against creditor claims.

Other methods may be used in the acquisition of a public company. One common way is the two-step acquisition. In step 1, the acquiring company makes a tender offer for 51 percent of the stock of the company being acquired, gaining enough stock ownership to obtain control. In step 2, it forms a new subsidiary (called the Acquisition Sub); the Acquisition Sub enters into a merger with the company being acquired, and the name of the merged company is changed to that of the company being acquired. The resulting company assumes all of the liabilities and assets of the previous company. This description leaves out many details relating to the merger, etc.

BASIC LEGAL CONCEPTS

Usually in step 2 of the transaction, the acquiring company attempts to get most of the remaining outstanding shares. If the acquirer has at least 90 percent of the shares in its control (counting the 51 percent it has already bought), the formalities of the merger are much simpler. Commonly, in step 1 the acquirer pays cash for the shares being acquired; in step 2, the additional shares acquired in connection with the merger are often acquired in a stock-for-stock exchange. The seller must pay capital gains tax in the stock-for-cash transaction. The seller normally does not have to pay capital gains tax in the stock-for-stock exchange, at least not until it sells the stock received in the exchange. Many sellers choose to sell some stock in the tender offer of step 1, and the rest of its stock in step 2. The two-step transaction satisfies the needs of different shareholders who have different cash needs; some shareholders have no immediate need for cash and would prefer to wait until the stock-for-stock exchange of step 2. Others need as much cash as possible up front, and don't wish to wait; they may even sell calls against the stock to be received in step 2, as a way of getting additional cash up front.

STATE UNIFORM STATUTES

BASIC LEGAL CONCEPTS

An important area of law consists of certain statutes drafted for adoption in all States. The most important and sweeping of these is the Uniform Commercial Code. This is because of the wide range of important topics covered by the code, ranging from matters relating to the sale of goods, to negotiable instruments such as promissory notes, checks, bonds, etc., to bank deposits and check collection, to creditors' rights, etc. This code may be supplemented in certain areas by Federal statutes. For example, the creditors' rights provisions are supplemented by the Federal bankruptcy code. The bank deposits and collections provisions are supplemented by Federal Reserve Regulation J, which is paramount as to the checks cleared through the Federal Reserve System. A huge proportion of the checks collected in the US are cleared through a check collection system set up under the leadership of the Federal Reserve Board and operated and maintained by the various Federal Reserve Banks.

REAL ESTATE: TITLE

The acceptability of the various kinds of title is determined by State and local statute and custom. In Arkansas, the most common forms of title are "warranty deed" and "quitclaim deed"; in the first of the two mentioned, the seller warrants that there is no defect in the title, going back to the beginning of time. In the latter case, the seller merely transfers whatever title he has to the property, warranting nothing. In New Jersey, the most common form of deed is "bargain and sale, with

BASIC LEGAL CONCEPTS

covenants against grantor". This is a step above a quitclaim deed, in that the seller agrees to be liable for any defects created by acts of the seller himself. For example, if a neighbor has encroached on the seller's property and he took no action to defend his property rights, the seller would be liable to the purchaser for any defect in title that was created.

Some people apparently think that all title questions can be left up to the title insurance company. Since title insurance is generally a requirement of the mortgage lender, the deal cannot go forward if the tile company won't insure. Therefore, assuming both buyer and seller want to do the deal, it is necessary for counsel for both sides be vigilant to ensure that the title company is not being arbitrary in denying coverage. When I bought my first house, the title company would not insure title because one of the four heirs of the owner of the house had not signed off on a sale of the property around 1910. The seller's attorney researched the law and facts and found that there was a foreclosure sale of the property in the 1930s, and that foreclosure sales absolutely bar any dispute over title arising as to matters occurring before the date of the foreclosure sale. This was demonstrated to the title company and the title company agreed to insure title.

REAL ESTATE: MORTGAGES

Most real estate purchases today are financed in large part by a mortgage. A first mortgage—which takes first priority over any other obligations with respect to the property—usually represents the bulk of the funds brought to the table at the

BASIC LEGAL CONCEPTS

purchase closing. First mortgages usually have fairly standardized terms and provisions. Most first mortgages have either a 15-year or a 30-year maturity. The rate on the mortgage may be a fixed rate, or an adjustable rate. The adjustable rate usually rests every year, based on the rate accruing on one-year government bonds. The adjustable rate mortgage sometimes has a fixed rate for a certain term of years, such as 5 years or seven years, and then adjusts every year after that.

Second mortgages are second only to a first mortgage on the property. The maturity is generally 10 or 15 years. Often, a seller in a real estate transaction will take back a "purchase money mortgage", which is really a second mortgage on the property being sold. Instead of the seller receiving all cash for his property in a sale, the seller receives mostly cash and an obligation of the buyer to pay a certain sum of money over a period of years, with this obligation secured by a second mortgage on the property. Many banks that provide first mortgage financing have a ban on purchase money mortgages in their term sheets for a first mortgage, even though the purchase money mortgage would be second to their first mortgage. The reasoning is that the payment obligation on the purchase money mortgage weakens the ability to pay on the first mortgage.

Technically, a mortgage financing consists of two separate instruments, one, a promissory note setting forth the terms of the obligation to pay, and second, a mortgage instrument granting the lender a security interest in the property that secures the obligation to pay. The mortgage instrument is recorded in whatever local clerk's office deeds of property are recorded in.

BASIC LEGAL CONCEPTS

There may also be other payment obligations secured by a lien on the property. The most common is a so-called "mechanic's lien". This arises when a workman does work on the property—such as an electrician or a plumber—and has not been paid. The workman can file a lien on the property for the amount he is owed. Another form of lien may arise when a creditor goes to court and gets a judgment against the property owner, and a "judgment lien" is filed on the property.

EXCHANGES OF "LIKE-KIND" INCOME PROPERTY ON A TAX-DEFERRED BASIS

Under section 1031 of the Internal Revenue Code, properties may be exchanged without triggering an immediate capital gains tax if they are of "like-kind". The exchange is not tax-free, as tax is merely deferred until a future transaction. Both the property exchanged and the property acquired must be used for a productive purpose in trade or business, or as an investment. Note that the real estate involved can be a single family residence that the owner holds as a rental property, so long as he does not use the property as his principal residence. To be of

BASIC LEGAL CONCEPTS

like kind, both properties must be domestic; a foreign property is not considered of "like kind."

In most cases, the property exchanged is of lesser or equal value to the property acquired, and the seller rolls his equity from one property into another. In exchanges in which the property exchanged is of greater value than the property acquired, cash must be exchanged to equalize the values. This cash is called "boot", and the boot is taxed at normal capital gains rates. (There are some further complications in exchanges in which the boot given is in the form of equipment or other property, and not all cash.)

The property owner must follow specific timing guidelines and other regulations to avoid capital gains taxation. Under current guidelines, the owner has 45 days in which to identify the replacement property, and 180 days in which to complete the exchange. It is also essential that a 1031 specialist, known as a Qualified Intermediary or Accommodator, be retained to hold the funds from the sale of the first property in trust or escrow until the exchange transaction is completed.

This 1031 rule applies only to income real estate and not to stocks and bonds. As we saw in an earlier section, an acquisition of a company made on a stock-for-stock basis may also be free of capital gains tax under separate rules.

BASIC LEGAL CONCEPTS

INTELLECTUAL PROPERTY

Many people, including many lawyers, think that the protection of intellectual property date back only to the adoption of the US Constitution and grant of authority to enact laws regulating patents and copyrights and to create the Patent and Trademark Office. In reality, intellectual property law came into the American law through a different route. The British Statute of Anne (1710) [regulating copyrights] and the Statute of Monopolies (1623) [regulating patents] became a part of British common law prior to the American Revolution (and prior to the Constitution). In each of the States in the new nation, the common law was "received" into the State law through the adoption of a Reception statute. Originally, the term patent had a different meaning than it does in modern usage; it originally meant the grant by the Crown of an **exclusive** right to the holder of a patent to engage in a particular activity. Thus, the British East India Company was granted a patent to exclusively engage in trading with the Indian States and principalities. Later, the term was used to refer only to the exclusive rights granted to an inventor to handle the production and sale of the product he had invented.

Under a French law of 1791, an author or an inventor was given the exclusive right to the financial benefit of his creation. This law, essentially contemporaneous with the US Constitution, also had a major influence on our conception of law in this area. With the creation of the North German Confederation in the 1860s, the term "intellectual property" came into legal existence as referring to this area of law. Today, there is a World Intellectual Property Organization (WIPO), an agency of

BASIC LEGAL CONCEPTS

the United Nations, which exists to coordinate legislation in this area. The usage of the term did not become common in the US until the last 30 years, although the term was used in a decision of the Massachusetts Supreme Judicial Court in 1845.

A patent is a grant of a property right to an invention, generally for a term of 20 years. In rare circumstances, extensions may be granted to the patent. A copyright is form of protection granted for "original works of authorship" of works of a literary, musical, artistic, dramatic or other intellectual nature. A trademark is a word, name, symbol, or device used in trade to distinguish one's goods from others' goods. All three are protected by actions taken by the US Patent and Trademark Office, by registration and by granting a property right. Trademarks have a long history under the common law outside the USPTO. My ancestor (also named John Ferrell), was granted a "mark" in 1682 in the Maryland colony, giving him the right to make a distinctive mark on the ears of his cattle.

A patent may be granted under the statute for the discovery or invention of "any new and useful process, machine, manufacture, or composition of matter," or "any new and useful improvements thereof." Note the two key words, "new" and "useful". There is a great deal of legal interpretation of the meanings of these two words. You may have a truly new and interesting invention, but if does not have a useful purpose, it cannot be patented.

Only the inventor may apply for a patent—not the money man or some other interested party. The inventor may have the assistance of a patent attorney or patent agent. Only a duly qualified and registered patent attorney or patent agent may appear before the USPTO in representing a client in regard to a

BASIC LEGAL CONCEPTS

patent. The agency has extensive and highly specific requirements regarding the science courses must have taken in college to be a registered agent or attorney, but nothing on the legal qualifications of a patent attorney. This does nothing to assure the legal competence of the inventor's representative, even if the representative was a science wonk in college.

The USPTO does not register copyrights. They are registered by the Copyright Office of the Library of Congress.

BASIC LEGAL CONCEPTS

RAISING EQUITY FOR BUSINESS

The Congress has directed the SEC to adopt rules for eliminating the prohibitions on general solicitation for investors and general advertising of offering of securities for securities being offered under Section 506 of Regulation D of the SEC or resales of securities under Rule 144A. Attached as Attachment A is a Fact Sheet describing the Congressional Act [the Jumpstart Our Business Startups Act] and the SEC actions in response thereto. For offerings under Reg. D sec. 506, the shares can only be offered to so-called "accredited investors", which the SEC has defined as meeting certain income and net worth requirements. Congress chose the name of the Act to make it the JOBS Act, reflecting the thought that easing the rules on raising capital for smaller enterprises would create jobs. It is still to be seen whether this will work. The SEC has not yet fully implemented the Act. In August 2012, it proposed new rules under the Act, but they have not been adopted. The proposal has received a large number of comments and objections; at this point, it is anybody's guess as to how the rules will finally turn out. It does not make sense at this point to devote much time and attention to the rules. Suffice it to say that these rules should be very important to efforts in the future to raise equity capital.

BASIC LEGAL CONCEPTS

DEBT CAPITAL

There are a multitude of ways of financing businesses on a short-term basis, such as for financing building of inventory. These include commercial paper, bankers' acceptances, factoring, loans from commercial finance companies, etc. Debt financing on a longer-term basis is often called debt capital.

Debt capital is usually either bonds or syndicated loans. Traditionally, bonds are used when the borrower wishes to use using a standard form instrument and enable it to be sold it to others. Traditionally, loans were more customized documents that were not generally resold. Nowadays, a syndicated loan is designed to be resold by the agent-lender to a variety of other lenders in a so-called syndicate or group. The loan documentation is fairly standardized and there is a loan trading association that prescribes standard form for trading a syndicated loan to another institution. Since the instrument of transfer and the loan itself has become standardized, it is hard to see a reason why a bond should be subject to regulation under the securities laws and a syndicated loan is generally not.

BASIC LEGAL CONCEPTS

SECURITIES TRANSFERS

Stocks and bonds are usually transferable by endorsement by the owner and delivery to the assignee. [One exception is "bearer bonds", which transfer simply by delivery without any endorsement; US Government-issued bonds are treated essentially like cash currency.] However, although endorsement and delivery are enough as between the owner and the assignee, as against the issuing corporation for dividend and voting purposes registration of the transfer on the books of the corporation

BASIC LEGAL CONCEPTS

is necessary to finish the transfer. If there are any restrictions on transfer, the restrictions must be noted prominently on the certificate to be effective.

When stock is transferred, the old share certificate should be cancelled and a new share certificate should be issued. The old certificate is cancelled by writing "cancelled" across the face of the certificate

To protect themselves against liability for improperly registering a transfer or improperly refusing to register a transfer, a corporation will usually employ a third party to act as transfer agent. Banks often act as transfer agents.

Sometimes the signature of the endorser must be "guaranteed" by a bank or brokerage firm which is familiar with the endorser's signature.

Virtually all shares are registered in the name of a nominee of the Depositary Trust Company or of a nominee of a brokerage firm. Although one can still register shares in the true owner's name, this is discouraged by the brokerage industry because administratively it is easier to effect transfers if the shares are held in one of the nominee names. Few legal issues arise regarding stock transfers any more.

BASIC LEGAL CONCEPTS

Attachment A

FACT SHEET

Eliminating the Prohibition on General Solicitation and General Advertising in Certain Offerings

Background

The Current Offering Process

Companies seeking to raise capital through the sale of securities must either register the securities offering with the SEC or rely on an exemption from registration. Most of the SEC's exemptions from registration prohibit companies from engaging in a general solicitation or general advertising in connection with securities offerings – that is, advertising in newspapers or on the Internet among other things. Rule 506 is one of those exemptions.

JOBS Act

The JOBS Act, enacted earlier this year, directed the SEC to remove the prohibitions on general solicitation or general advertising for securities offerings relying on Rule 506. By requiring the SEC to remove these restrictions, Congress sought to make it easier for companies to inform the public that they are seeking to raise capital through the sale of securities.

In particular, Section 201(a)(1) of the JOBS Act directs the SEC to amend Rule 506 to permit general solicitation or

BASIC LEGAL CONCEPTS

general advertising provided that all purchasers of the securities are accredited investors. It also says that "[s]uch rules shall require the issuer to take reasonable steps to verify that purchasers of the securities are accredited investors, using such methods as determined by the Commission."

The new law also directs the SEC to revise Rule 144A, which governs the resale of securities primarily by larger institutional investors known as qualified institutional buyers (QIBs). Under current Rule 144A, offers of securities can only be made to QIBs. Under the new law, Rule 144A would be revised so that offers of securities could be made to investors who are not QIBs as long as the securities are sold only to persons whom the seller reasonably believes are QIBs.

The Proposed Rules

Rule 506

Under the proposed rules, companies issuing securities would be permitted to use general solicitation and general advertising to offer securities, provided that:

- The issuer takes reasonable steps to verify that the purchasers of the securities are accredited investors.
- All purchasers of securities are accredited investors, because either:
    - They come within one of the categories of persons who are accredited investors under existing Rule 501.
    - The issuer reasonably believes that they meet one of the categories at the time of the sale of the securities.

BASIC LEGAL CONCEPTS

Under Rule 501, a natural person qualifies as an accredited investor if he or she has individual net worth – or joint net worth with a spouse – that exceeds $1 million at the time of the purchase, excluding the value of the primary residence of such person. Or, if he or she has income exceeding $200,000 in each of the two most recent years or joint income with a spouse exceeding $300,000 for those years and a reasonable expectation of the same income level in the current year.

In determining the reasonableness of the steps that an issuer has taken to verify that a purchaser is an accredited investor, the proposing release explains that issuers are to consider the facts and circumstances of the transaction. This includes, among other things, the following factors:

- The type of purchaser and the type of accredited investor that the purchaser claims to be.
- The amount and type of information that the issuer has about the purchaser.
- The nature of the offering, meaning:
    o The manner in which the purchaser was solicited to participate in the offering.
    o The terms of the offering, such as a minimum investment amount.

The SEC's proposing release notes that proposing specific verification methods that an issuer must use "would be impractical and potentially ineffective in light of the numerous ways in which a purchaser can qualify as an accredited investor ... We are also concerned that a prescriptive rule that specifies required verification methods could be overly burdensome in some cases, by requiring issuers to follow the same steps, regardless of their particular circumstances, and ineffective in others, by

BASIC LEGAL CONCEPTS

requiring steps that, in the particular circumstances, would not actually verify accredited investor status."

The proposed rules would preserve the existing portions of Rule 506 as a separate exemption so that companies conducting 506 offerings without the use of general solicitation and general advertising would not be subject to the new verification rule.

Rule 144A

Under the proposed rules, securities sold pursuant to Rule 144A could be offered to persons other than QIBs, including by means of general solicitation, provided that the securities are sold only to persons whom the seller and any person acting on behalf of the seller reasonably believe is a QIB.

Form D

The proposed rules would amend Form D, which issuers must file with the SEC when they sell securities under Regulation D. The revised form would add a separate box for issuers to check if they are claiming the new Rule 506 exemption that would permit general solicitation and general advertising.

http://www.sec.gov/news/press/2012/2012-170.htm

Home | Previous Page

www.ingramcontent.com/pod-product-compliance
Lightning Source LLC
Chambersburg PA
CBHW071551170526
45166CB00004B/1628